How to Become
a Chef

The Essential Guide
for Becoming a Chef
and Building a Successful
Culinary Career

by Brandon Fiore

Table of Contents

Introduction

Of all the reasons for which you might harbor ambitions of becoming a chef, because of the relentlessly-demanding nature of the culinary industry, you must first be honest with yourself and make sure you're truly passionate about cooking. If you don't have a real passion for what you should be viewing as an art (culinary art), you'll quickly become frustrated along the journey, which will seriously hamper your chances of career advancement.

If you are indeed passionate about cuisine, and if you can see yourself consistently cooking up a storm for prolonged periods of time, then becoming a chef may seem like a natural step to take in an attempt to formalize your culinary interest and hopefully turn it into a rewarding career. Besides your undying passion for the culinary world, other reasons for which you might want to be a chef encompass the very real possibility of a great salary that you'd earn doing what you love, an excellent opportunity for career advancement, and very positive job-growth projections.

In theory, the process of becoming a chef can be approached from a variety of different ways, one of which requires very little or basic formal education and training. In reality however, as a result of the positive growth prospects tied to becoming a chef, this career path and its subsequent industry is becoming more and more competitive. This ever increasing competitiveness is making it harder and harder for aspiring chefs to realize any real career advancement without formal culinary education and training; so taking the time to get formally trained and educated is a great starting point if you do want to advance in your culinary career. In fact, you should consider it mandatory if you are planning on climbing the ladder to work your way up.

As a relatively well-established chef, your career opportunities won't only be limited to the restaurant industry. Every aspiring chef probably has at least one or two signature dishes they've either created themselves, or adapted in their own unique way. Getting to a stage in your culinary career where you can exercise the freedom to develop new menus and dishes is almost impossible without first building the kind of credentials that start with some sort of standardized formal culinary education. You have to be armed with all the right information, however, because what is very quickly growing into an opportunity-rich industry is not immune to opportunism. You can very easily become overwhelmed with the seemingly endless requirements you're expected to fulfill in the quest to becoming a qualified chef, which is exactly why this book was written: to clarify the path to becoming a chef.

Read on to learn exactly how to become a chef, where and how to get started, the cost and time commitment requirements, where to get a job once suitably qualified, and how to advance in your culinary career and move up the ladder, - assuming your ambition is to soon become an executive (head) chef. You will also be provided with other valuable information about how to pursue a rewarding career as a chef despite career-limiting challenges, such as the lack of adequate funds to finance your culinary schooling requirements, and how to pursue resource-intensive employment opportunities.

Chapter 1: Training and Qualification Requirements

It's understandably very tempting to try and get into the culinary field without any formal training or education, especially because it is indeed possible. You *can* definitely start from the very bottom (perhaps as a waiter in exceptional cases) and work your way up the culinary ladder in your specific work environment, but it must be emphasized that this would be a very long shot. Furthermore, in an increasingly competitive market and industry, the best culinary jobs aspired to by the most ambitious and best chefs almost always go to chefs whose credentials go beyond practical experience. The knowledgebase of a top chef who gets considered for top culinary positions should resemble that of someone who demonstrates a broad understanding of food that spreads beyond the actual food itself.

Knowing how the food is prepared, served and perhaps its cultural and geographic origins is pretty much the basics of what you need to know as a chef. If you want to set yourself apart however, and enjoy the prospect of real career advancement, your knowledge and experience with food needs to go way beyond that; something which can only be truly attained with formal culinary education. A formal culinary education in a sense opens your eyes up to the many possibilities associated with the culinary arts, all the while giving you a solid grounding in the standards and basics of the industry. With the solid grounding and basics covered, it then becomes your decision in which direction to take your career.

You can decide to go on and specialize in a specific range or type of food, for example serving and even developing Gourmet dishes which are served to an exclusive selection of fine-dining guests.

Getting qualified will also make your job-hunting quest that much easier—so much easier in fact than you might ever have thought without any formal culinary education.

Basic & Prerequisite Knowledge

We've already established that prior to pursuing a career in the culinary arts, you simply have to have an interest in or passion for cooking. If you can confirm that you do indeed have an interest in the culinary arts, you will already have endeavored to broaden your knowledge of the culinary arts, however informal your efforts to broaden that knowledge may have been. If you find yourself following up on a cooking show you've watched by doing further research on how a particular dish is prepared, how many variations it has, where it originated from and perhaps even some technical details about its ingredients, you definitely have the makings of a dynamic and ever-progressive chef destined for a great career. This further highlights the need for you to be passionate about the culinary arts because the most important part of formalizing your culinary education entails your ability to grasp the process of creating a dish, together with the subsequent gastronomic experience around what leaves your kitchen. Your desire and aptitude to learn and refine the process pretty much covers all the prerequisite knowledge you'll need to formally pursue your culinary education.

Culinary Training Institutions (Culinary Schools)

Depending on the level and depth at which you desire to get formally educated as a chef, the culinary school options range from online cooking courses and casual (on-demand) cooking classes right up to cooking courses offered in universities and community colleges. Some of the most highly-esteemed culinary schools include specialist culinary institutions, such as the Culinary Institute of America, the French Culinary Institute, and the Johnson and Wales University (College of Culinary Arts).

Prestige and high-esteem aside, one of the main factors which will naturally determine your choice of the institution where you're going to get your formal culinary education is indeed finances. This is not to say that if you can't afford to get educated and trained at one of the most prestigious culinary schools your career prospect and advancement prospects are limited. With regards to formal culinary education, it's all about what you take away from the curriculum and, more importantly, what you aim to do with what you have earned. Attending one of the most prestigious culinary institutes doesn't guarantee you anything and it certainly doesn't guarantee you positive career advancement. A Johnson & Wales Degree in the Culinary Arts is a mega boost for your chances of ultimately realizing that dream of one day becoming an executive chef, but the degree alone doesn't guarantee that eventuality. In fact, with the right approach, even those who take cooking classes online can strategically work their way up the ladder, navigate the industry and ultimately realize their dream of becoming a head chef.

All of that said however, if your finances are in good order, your best bet is to go through formal culinary training at a prestigious culinary institution such as Johnson and Wales, the Culinary Institute of America or the French Culinary Institute. Others factors which will come into play will obviously include things like how much time you have on your hands (can you commit to a four-year, full time degree?), whether you need to start earning some money as a chef in the immediate future, and your proximity to the culinary school campus you wish to attend. The French Culinary Institute for example is located in New York City, while the Culinary Institute of America offers a choice of three locations, namely New York, California and Texas. The Culinary institute of America also has a campus in Singapore which is indicative of the variation offered by many culinary institutions and shines a light on another aspect of pursuing a career as a chef—the prospect of your work taking you all over the world. The different careers in their abundance will be discussed in detail in the next chapter.

Essentially, it's up to you at which institutions you're going to pursue your formal training and education to become a chef. This doesn't mean that absolutely any entity offering culinary education and training will do. In order to be competent as a chef, especially one seeking career advancement prospects, you have to have some basic knowledge of the culinary arts considered to be standard. This brings us to the curriculum:

Culinary Training Curriculum

As previously touched-on, how well you'll do beyond the classroom depends on what you take away from your training. What ultimately matters is how you fare in the high-pressure cooker that is the culinary working environment, and how consistently you deliver great results. Being average just doesn't cut it for chefs, especially for those seeking to make their way up the ladder and ultimately have the authority of an executive chef.

Whichever institutional avenue you choose to pursue for your culinary school education, make sure you have a solid grasp of the essentials of working in a kitchen, extending the services to encompass the entire dining experience and conventions such as specific or best dishes for a particular season, culinary theme or geographical/cultural convention. A solid culinary school curriculum also covers aspects such as competence in using food preparation tools (knife skills), stock and sauce preparation, distinguishing the quality of food products and ingredients, technical details about common seasonings, working environment (kitchen) management, palate development and important standard cooking techniques (Asian, Latin, and American regional culinary techniques).

The official curriculum offered at your culinary school of choice may not name their modules exactly like the above, but that pretty much covers what the standard curriculum should entail to standardize your knowledge. This is where budding chefs attending certain culinary schools triumph over others, in that some culinary institutions go the extra mile and cover subjects such as the business side of the culinary arts.

Keeping in mind that despite the huge advantage formal culinary education offers, at some point in your career, you'll have to get down to the actual cooking and physically demonstrate your skills. That said, education is extremely important if you want to give yourself the best chance at advancing in the industry. Something else to remember is that you don't have to be a particularly talented cook in order to enjoy a great career as a successful chef. Success as a chef comes down to your ability to learn and apply what you've learned in practice. There are many people who have a natural affinity with all things culinary, but it takes way more than that to become a chef.

If you have a passion for cooking and you're willing to learn, where you get your training and education is almost insignificant. The more practical your culinary learning curriculum is, however, the better, because practical experience will eventually emerge as the most defining factor of your career as a chef. Keeping this in mind, you would not ideally get your culinary education via platforms such as online programs. The market prefers practical experience driven by a deep-running knowledgebase of the culinary world.

Some culinary institutions have extended prerequisites if you wish to enroll with them, such as the Culinary Institute of America. You have to be employed for at least a six-month period working in the kitchen of an establishment not serving fast food before enrolling with them. This only serves to further emphasize the practical, hands-on nature of working in the culinary industry as a chef. Such prerequisites are also a great way to offer prospective chefs a window into the taxing realities of working in what is a high-pressure environment and industry.

Types of Culinary School Qualifications

As far as qualifications go, at the end of your culinary schooling, you can walk away with either an official qualification such as a Degree or Associate Degree in Culinary Arts (Culinary Arts BA, Culinary Art AS, Art of Cooking AS), a Culinary Arts Certificate. You can also obtain an unofficial certificate, which can carry just as much weight as a formal qualification in the market. Such unofficial certificates only carry weight depending on where you obtain them from, and identifying such institutions or establishments that offer such certification requires your own initiative. A certified cooking course offered by the industry's employers, such as well-known restaurants or chefs, may carry just as much weight as the formal culinary training offered by a prestigious school. However, this is subjective.

Chapter 2: How Much Will It Cost?

Although this shouldn't ideally be the case, the reality is that most peoples' entry into the culinary industry is dictated by finances, particularly with regards to where you plan to complete your culinary schooling. This chapter will cover the basic cost estimates of not only going through culinary school and getting a formal culinary education, but also what other options you have if you want to pursue a career as a chef (if you don't have the money to put yourself through school or explore geographically-challenging employment opportunities).

Generic Culinary School Costs

While the exact costs of attending a culinary school course will naturally differ depending on the institution you're attending, the costs involved aren't only limited to the tuition fees. You will have to consider and factor in costs such as administrative (application) fees, supply fees for books and cooking tools, commuting fees (if applicable) and your day-to-day living expenses. Indicatively, the cheapest culinary training programs are those which can be taken online, but they are generally not as highly-regarded as the more hands-on courses. Online culinary courses for chefs specifically can cost anything up to around $2,000–$3,000, but it's normally way less than that.

The next affordable (and perhaps better) option of a culinary school is either a local community or city college, which typically never costs more than $5,000 in tuition and study material (prescribed books).

For those who do have the budget to pursue their culinary education through a full-service or specialist culinary school, such as those offered at a private culinary institute or college/university, costs range anywhere from around $6,000 right up to $35,000–$45,000. Factors that add to the variable total costs largely depend on your level of specialization, something which is encouraged if you ultimately want to pursue a specific culinary path as a specialized chef. If you really want to save without compromising the quality of the education you desire, choosing the right culinary school comes down to finding one from which you can get some real value—value you can build on while you work in the industry beyond your formal studies. Sometimes the prestige of a culinary school is the only reason behind the seemingly high cost of the culinary courses they offer.

When You Don't Have the Funds to Finance Your Studies

For those who don't have a single cent to finance their culinary schooling, general and freely available culinary knowledge is available at the click of a mouse button, and you can learn everything there is to know about all things culinary by simply conducting research. However, you have to develop a knack for separating good, reliable information from a lot of the junk that is out there. You can very easily run an online search to learn how to prepare a certain dish, culinary style or even learn about presentation. Starting out a career as a chef requires the ability to implement what you learn and put it into practice, so your research and self-education should be accompanied by a foray into the culinary market. You can apply for a job in the cooking industry even if you only have a basic high school education—just be sure to demonstrate the ability and willingness to learn and improve.

One of the greatest ways to launch your career as chef with very limited resources is to establish yourself as a cooking authority. The online space serves as the ultimate platform through which to do this, explored through blogging or vlogging (posting cooking videos, preferably of you demonstrating your ability to adhere to sought-after cooking standards), all while raising money through tools such as pay-per-click adverts placed on your blog or website. What you should do is demonstrate your dynamism as a chef that never stops learning, all the while broadening your knowledgebase and perhaps even earning advertising and affiliate revenue through your online platform. This is a great way to carve out a culinary career for yourself, without relying on anyone to employ you directly.

Another avenue to explore if you don't have the finances to kick start your culinary career is that of applying for a scholarship or bursary. This obviously applies only to those who seek to receive formal culinary school education, but there's a trick to it. As with anything else, there are undoubtedly numerous applicants competing for the same scholarship as you are, so you have to be very tactful about how you go about filling out your application. Financial aid in the form of scholarships or bursaries is awarded to prospects that prove themselves to be good candidates for a good return on investment. If a creditor gives you a loan (even in the form of a scholarship or bursary), their final decision to give you the loan is based on whether they perceive you as a debtor who has the ability to make good on their loan and eventually pay back the money lent to them one way or the other.

In the case of the culinary industry, the question comes down to whether you're going to be able to land the job you're studying or training for once your schooling has ended.

The trick that will make you a great final candidate is your demonstrated ability to make good on the bursar's investment in you. In your cover letter, include a report that covers how you went to various employers in the industry and spoke to them about your job prospects if you were to finish the proposed culinary course, for which you require funding, and then go back for immediate employment. You will of course have to complete what you've promised and truthfully report on the actual outcome.

Keep in mind that there are various other costs involved in the process of pursuing a career as a chef—costs which aren't only limited to culinary school tuition fees. All of these costs should be considered, some of which take the form of having to hand in your resume in person or showing up for a face-to-face interview, etc. In summary, the various avenues through which you can become a chef can cost from nothing more than what you pay for your Internet bandwidth up to $45,000 and more in some cases.

Chapter 3: Scoring a Job as a Chef

If the process of applying for a job as a chef doesn't exhaust you, you're simply not trying hard enough. The culinary industry is no easier than any other industry, but with the right effort you can land a good job with great prospects of career advancement.

There should be no online job opening, related to the culinary field, to which you haven't applied. You definitely don't want to be short on options and put yourself in a position where the very first job offer is the one you snap up immediately. What you want to have is a long list of options to choose from because then you'd be able to weigh each offer up against the other and ultimately settle on the one that's best for you in a number of ways. You could have an offer for a job requiring you to commute an extra mile or two, for example, jobs with a higher pay package might cost you more in travel expenses when compared to a lower-paying job that's only a short walking distance away.

Cast your net wide and leave no stone unturned. Some advertised vacancies (especially the ones online) aren't even real, but there's no way of knowing which ones are and which ones aren't, so apply anyway.

Applying online also puts you in direct contact with culinary jobs in different geographic locations, so if you have ambitions of working abroad, the only way to land such a job is running an online job search.

Take to the Streets

Once you've combed the Internet for all jobs related to your industry (and applied), multiply your job-search impact by knocking on doors. Physically go to culinary establishments such as restaurants, hotels, cruise companies, casinos, buffets, catering companies, etc. and offer your services. Hand in your resume directly to the highest authority and ask them in-person whether they have a job for you.

If you put in this amount of effort you'll have offers in no time. The culinary industry follows a trend which might become apparent to you if you take the time to look a little closer, it is the fact that chefs usually change jobs twice before they settle on the culinary establishment with which they feel their career has the best chance of advancing. Your first job doesn't have to be your last, so you can definitely settle for low-paying job at first, if only for the experience. If feasible, you can even volunteer your services for a while, as experience is simply invaluable for any aspiring chef.

Creating a Chef Job for Yourself

Getting employed as a chef doesn't have to mean relying on an employer handing you a job—you can explore alternative avenues such as opening a mobile food-trailer which specializes in your culinary specialty. If you don't have the required start-up capital, approach a culinary establishment such as a local restaurant and talk to the owner/manager about extending their reach through a mobile food trailer that you'll be happy to run.

Chapter 4: Advancing Your Career to Executive Chef

Fortunately for anyone seeking to land a job as a chef, job growth prospects look very good, even depicting signs of further growth. With the right kind of effort mentioned in the previous chapter, you will eventually land a job as a chef, but it might not be quite at the level you ultimately desire.

It's only natural for dynamic chefs to want to advance their career and climb the culinary career ladder to ultimately hold the title of executive or head chef. Because established chefs tend to hold their executive positions for a relatively long time, however, working your way up the ladder requires some strategic insight. Simply working to stand out in a particular kitchen may not be enough to earn you that jump to your coveted head chef position, in which case you have to be very strategic about changing the establishment you work for.

As with any industry, standing out with the aim of obtaining a promotion requires all the usual clichés such as hard work, dedication, an undying passion, and perhaps taking the initiative to demonstrate your desire to make the leap. If you have an established head chef or even a queue of established executive chef prospects ahead of you based on considerations such as experience or time spent working with the same establishment, the usual clichés aren't enough for you to advance in the way you desire.

The makings of an executive chef are grounded on their ability to manage the staff around them, in addition to a deep-running and extensive knowledge of the industry. If you do indeed want to take your destiny of eventually becoming an executive chef into your own hands, forget the usual itinerary of working your way up one establishment with the aim of getting noticed and progressively promoted.

Often all it takes to get exactly what you want is simply asking for it. What harm can it do if you already know that the answer is going to be "no"? Obviously you'll have to garner some experience under your belt and refine your abilities, skills and knowledge—you can't realistically expect to be made executive chef after only a couple of years in the industry. What you *should* do is work hard in whatever position you currently hold, at the same time constantly identifying new opportunities. These new opportunities can include the likes of other restaurants that are expanding, opening new branches or completely new restaurants set to open. Apply to such opportunities in your "growing capacity" as a prospective head chef that is 'stuck' in an establishment that limits your ambitions and growing ability. Don't bash or be negative towards your current employers though—all you want to do is demonstrate your desire and ability to advance in your career and "take your rightful place" in an environment that has the space allowing you to do so.

One last strategy to implement is changing jobs. Yes, you have to change jobs at least twice in order to build up a positive track record. Each time you do, try to solicit some positive feedback from your former employers and colleagues. Regret letters of former employees expressing their sadness of loosing you work best, and a series of this positive feedback creates the impression that you're in constant search of greener pastures (executive chef position). This should be implemented in conjunction with some strategic networking—getting in touch with as many head chefs as you can, particularly older ones on the brink of retirement and trying to get them to recommend you as a possible successor.

The head chef position will not be sitting there waiting for you—you have to actively seek it out and at times fend off criticism for attempting to get the position.

Chapter 5: Customizing Your Culinary Career-Path Plan

The previous chapters collectively covered the typical steps which entail one's pursuit of a culinary career as a chef, including training and qualification requirements, the costs involved, how long it takes to acquire the required skills or certification, how to go about finding a job, and how to pursue any ambitions of advancing your career to executive or head chef level. Practically pursuing your career on the road to becoming a chef poses a lot of different challenges in practice though. Depending on your unique set of circumstances, such as where you live, your financial situation, how quickly you want or need to start working and earning, and many others, you have to tailor your path to becoming a chef.

There isn't a one-size-fits-all path—something you've probably discovered by now—because it doesn't make sense for you to enroll in a non-paying, exclusively educational culinary course that is in a different state if you have an immediate need to start earning an income, for example. In the same way, an aspiring chef who has all the money required to complete a culinary degree would be wasting much-needed study time by deciding to also hold down a demanding cooking job to earn money. Ultimately, it all comes down to what your specific needs and circumstances are, but we'll go through a few possible scenarios you might find yourself in, with regards to how you should approach your quest to becoming a chef, and match those with a culinary career-path plan.

On your journey to becoming a chef, something else you'll also discover is the fact that there are some areas along your career path where you'll have to compromise. For instance, your ultimate plan for your culinary career might be to have your Culinary Arts college degree completed in the standard four-year period and then perhaps giving yourself another five years to make it to your ultimate position of being an executive chef. In this instance, various factors may come into play, forcing you to compromise a bit and alter some elements. You might have to spend an extra year in college or have to get a part-time job to keep up with increasing living costs. Whatever it is you might have to compromise on, never compromise on the end-goal. In this particular example, you can compromise on the total time spent to eventually become an executive chef, but never compromise on the desire (to be an executive) itself.

Scenario 1—You're just out of high school and you're ready to formalize your love affair with the culinary arts, so you want to study to be a chef and get some extensive academic knowledge of the field before entering the job market:

In this case, your best bet would be a four-year college, university or culinary institute course as this gives you ample time to gain experience while studying. Unless you need to bring in money immediately, don't worry about getting a paid part-time job at this stage—just worry about beefing up your culinary knowledge as extensively as possible. A two-year culinary course might also be a great starting point, but if you can, go the full nine yards.

Scenario 2—You've been active in a totally different industry, pursuing what is increasingly becoming an unfulfilling career and you want to make the jump from your current career into a dynamic career as a chef:

In this case, apply the principles of advancing your career as explored in the previous chapter (changing jobs and demonstrating your growing ability to become an ideal executive chef). Just make sure you have another job lined up before executing the jump, and make sure you leave a good track record behind (leaving your previous job on a good note).

Scenario 3—You're already active in the food and restaurant industry, but you feel as if the only way you can advance within the industry and perhaps one day become executive/head chef is if you formalized your knowledge of the industry through formal culinary training/qualification:

In this case you might have to be prepared to either take a pay-cut and work fewer hours, or try exploring a full-time culinary education. If you're in this situation, your prospects are probably more positive than you might initially think because based on the amount of practical work experience you have by now, you're an ideal candidate to get funding for your studies by way of a full or partial bursary/scholarship. In some cases, the culinary establishment you already work for might even be willing to fund your education. A two-year course through which you get a culinary certificate would probably be the best option, but if you can put in the right amount of commitment

and go back to the pay that matches that of a student,
a four-year culinary degree is a great consideration.

Conclusion

Your decision to become a chef should really be based on only ONE consideration—the passion you have for cooking. If you don't have a real passion for cooking, you won't last in what is a very high-pressure working environment and overall competitive industry.

Getting a formal education and undergoing formal training isn't an explicit requirement for becoming a chef, but it goes a very long way in broadening your culinary career prospects for advancement, especially if you have ambitions of one day holding the title of executive or head chef. If you're going to pursue an appropriate education by attending culinary school, the most expensive institutions aren't necessarily the very best, and sometimes these institutions are expensive only because of the prestige they carry.

Your formal culinary school education can be completed via a number of different channels, from the less fancied online classes to the ones which carry a bit more weight, like community colleges, universities and specialist institutions, such as culinary institutes.

With the right balance of theoretical knowledge and progressively built-up practical experience, you shouldn't have too many problems landing a job as a chef, but you'll have to put in the effort to apply and constantly be on the lookout for better opportunities. Do not limit your job search to online platforms however, because some of the best chef jobs are reserved for those who show their initiative by approaching hiring authorities directly.

Possessing the skills of a chef also opens up the door to a self-made career, through which you can earn money by establishing yourself as an authority and perhaps setting up an online cooking platform which you can monetize in a number of ways. You can also get discovered in this way and receive direct offers.

If you want to achieve career advancement and ultimately become a head chef, you have to take the initiative to capitalize on any opportunities that may present themselves in other culinary establishments, waiting to be pursued even while you're still working for a specific employer. Always leave a good legacy though, wherever you choose to go, and understand that it's very rare for chefs to work their way up to the executive chef position by staying with the very first culinary establishment that employed them.

Finally, I'd like to thank you for purchasing this book! If you found it helpful, I'd greatly appreciate it if you'd take a moment to leave a review on Amazon. Thank you!

Printed in Great Britain
by Amazon

12577138R00029